Precious Companion

A Book of Comfort and Remembrance
After the Loss of a Pet

Laynee Gilbert

 L.O.A. Publications

Cover and interior design by Patricia Krebs.

Layout by Marcie Gilbert and Patricia Krebs.

Original cover and interior photos © 2007 by Marcie Gilbert.

Additional photographs used with permission of Patricia Krebs, Germán Krebs and Ann Milligan Lees.

Continuation of permissions and acknowledgments on page 94.

First edition published 2007 by L.O.A. Publications.

L.O.A. Publications
P.O. Box 6107
San Jose, California 95150-6107
LOApubs@aol.com
www.loapublications.com

ISBN-10: 0-9678966-2-2
ISBN-13: 978-0-9678966-2-5

Other books by Laynee Gilbert:
Pass It On: Ultimate Reflections on Life and Death
I Remember You: A Grief Journal
The Complete Dream Journal

This Book is Dedicated
to the Memory of

_____

They did not love him for his glossy tiger coat,
nor for his white shirt front and white paws,
nor for his great green eyes,
no, not even for the white tip to his tail.
They loved him because he was himself.

May Sarton
The Fur Person

Precious Companion

Christopher woke late.
For just a second he didn't remember
the reason why a cold nose had not nudged him awake.
But the recollection of last night came rushing into the summer morning
and he knew that he would never see Bodger again.

Carol Carrick
The Accident

Your pet has died, and your heart aches.

To me, my pets are my children. When one dies, the loss is terribly painful, no matter how many have died before. When I adopt a pet, I take on the responsibility to love and care for this being till death do we part. Unlike human children, animal children are likely to die before their human parents. It's a tremendous emotional risk, because the pain of loss is inevitable. Those of us who take that risk again and again know it exists, but it doesn't make the pain any easier.

When a human family member dies, there is usually an abundance of sympathy and support. When a pet dies, rarely does anyone acknowledge the loss with more than a passing comment. Well-wishers recommend getting another pet as soon as possible to replace the deceased one, but there is no replacement. When a child dies, does another "replace" it? No. That is not to say that another child or pet is not a welcome addition to the family after a mourning period, but there can never be a "replacement."

As I write, my kits take turns walking across my keyboard, settling into my lap. Although one cannot predict with certainty, chances are these kits will also die before I do. I cannot dwell on this fact; just the thought brings painful grief I don't yet want or need to bear. Yet remembering the fragility and impermanence of life is important, a reminder not to take even a single moment with loved ones for granted.

On Grief

Days went by, and I couldn't seem to get over it. I couldn't eat. I couldn't sleep. I couldn't cry. I was all empty inside, but hurting. Hurting worse than I'd ever hurt in my life. Hurting with a sickness there didn't seem to be any cure for. Thinking every minute of my big yeller dog...

Fred Gipson
Old Yeller

Denial, numbness, anger, guilt, regret, sadness—and a thousand variations to each of these themes—are all emotions common to the grief experience. Feelings of powerlessness and helplessness abound. The most important thing you can do for yourself is to simply acknowledge all the thoughts and feelings *without judgment*. It's hard enough dealing with the judgments of others, those who believe it's "silly" to have such strong feelings for and attachments to animals. Honor your emotions with the same respect and compassion as you would honor a friend's.

Don't let anyone tell you how you *should* feel or how you *should* grieve. Every person grieves differently, and every loss is unique. Sometimes we think we need to prove our love by grieving in a certain way or for a certain amount of time. Be true to yourself. Trust your own path. Give yourself permission to express your pain in whatever way helps best. Cry, pound pillows, talk to a friend, write. You never know when a wave of grief will hit. Some of the waves may be for other losses that came before this one. Take time to write or talk about these other losses as well.

Just as we grieve, our surviving pets grieve as well. My kitty Shira was only a few months old when her big brother Kazi died, but in their short time together, they had become very close. Kazi was a very loving companion to Shira, and the two often curled up together for naps. Shortly after Kazi's death, Shira began to compulsively bathe herself. In fact, within a month's time she had managed to lick herself bald over nearly half of her body. The vet recommended a plastic neck guard that nearly killed her in her efforts to remove it. I finally realized that this behavior was actually a symptom of her own grief, and what she needed most was merely the space and time to get through it herself. After a few more weeks and a whole lot of special loving attention, she discontinued the behavior and eventually bonded very tightly with a new little brother.

Sometimes grief takes a long time, even years. Getting through grief doesn't mean we forget about the one we lost. It just means we can think about him or her without constantly being enveloped by pain. It means our happy memories stand out more than the unhappy ones. It means we can love again without guilt.

Trust the process of grief. It is truly nature's best remedy for a broken heart.

On Writing and Remembering

"I want to write a story about her."
She couldn't quite explain this sudden feeling. But somehow she knew
that if she could do this the hare would stay alive for her even after Harry
had shoveled the dark earth on top of the body.

Dennis Hamley
Hare's Choice

When you write in a book, you become part of that book, and it becomes part of you. When you write about your precious companion, the two of you become bound together in a unique and powerful way.

On the following pages, authors express love and grief for their beloved animal companions through prose, poetry, letters and stories. Become one of those authors yourself. Let their experiences inspire you to write about your own.

In the empty spaces between words and images, add your own valuable memories, feelings, thoughts and dreams. Paste a favorite photograph or two between the pages. Draw pictures and write poems. As you remember and reflect on your departed companion in these and other meaningful ways, you will be not only helping yourself to heal, but also creating a keepsake book of the one that brought so much joy into your life.

Your precious companion is gone, but the memories will live on.

Now turn the page, and begin filling the emptiness.

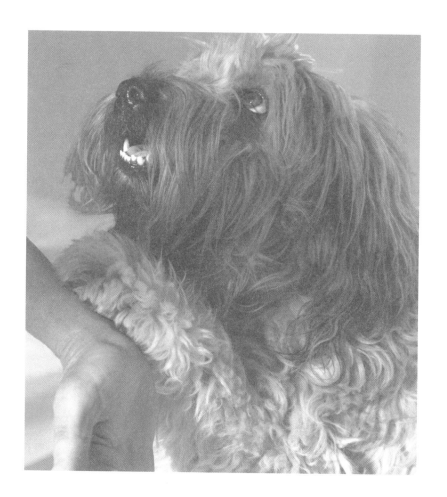

It was wonderful indeed how I could have heart-to-heart talks with my dogs and they always seemed to understand. Each question I asked was answered in their own doggish way.

Although they couldn't talk in my terms, they had a language of their own that was easy to understand. Sometimes I would see the answer in their eyes, and again it would be in the friendly wagging of their tails. Other times I could hear the answer in a low whine or feel it in the soft caress of a warm flicking tongue. In some way, they would always answer.

Wilson Rawls
Where the Red Fern Grows

Little Willy knelt down, took Searchlight by the ears, and looked directly into her eyes. She had the greenest eyes you've ever seen. "I won't ever give you away. Ever. I promise." He put his arms around the dog's strong neck and held her tightly. "I love you, Searchlight." And Searchlight understood, for she had heard those words many times before.

John Reynolds Gardiner
Stone Fox

Keesha was my friend, my confidant, my angel and, ultimately, my teacher.

Susan Chernak McElroy
Animals as Teachers & Healers

You're never too old to value that emotional safety and silent, consistent support from your pet. He becomes a sort of sanctuary for you after an argument or a stressful day at work, when your friends forget you or your spouse dies, when no words can comfort you or you just need someone to talk to. Because he gives without demanding much in return, you can easily consider him among the best of your friends and a secure companion.

Jamie Quackenbush
When Your Pet Dies

"I knew that she knew me. All the way through, like nobody else. And I didn't have to say anything."

Jan Slepian
The Broccoli Tapes

"He knew something was wrong, and, as he had all his life, he turned to me for help. But *there was nothing I could do*, and that devastated me."

Jamie Quackenbush
When Your Pet Dies

She couldn't let him suffer now because *she* didn't want him to die.

She couldn't keep on hurting him.

She couldn't be that selfish.

A.M. Monson
The Deer Stand

In what seemed just a few seconds it was all over. Dr. Tierney did a last check. "He's gone,"
he said quietly. Only then did I release my hugging hold, but, as I say, I still remember
that last effort of his, and I shall remember it always. I only hope that someday I
shall forget that part of my memory which tells me that I was part of doing
something wrong to him, but rather there will remain only the memory
that I was part of doing something which had to be done.

Cleveland Amory
The Best Cat Ever

Funny how some things don't get real until after.

It felt like pins and needles in my face and fingers, but I didn't cry.

Just everything stopped, my breath, my heart, my hearing, everything.

Jan Slepian
The Broccoli Tapes

I felt like a robot walking on the beach. Like a robot picking apples. Like a robot going to the movies. Not like my usual self. And I got scared. What if not just Whiskers died, but all my feelings along with her?

Doris Orgel
Whiskers Once and Always

Who has not experienced that special sense of awareness and greeting, when we put the key in the lock and open the door? Just coming home is a major event. We had become so used to anticipating our pet's welcome, from a meow or so to a tail-thumping salute. Now it is silent. But the pet's presence still seems everywhere. We now live in the echoes of the loving patterns that became our way of life.

Wallace Sife
The Loss of a Pet

I didn't know that when people talk about having a broken heart, that it's true.

That's what it feels like inside.

My heart hurts.

Everything hurts,

even my bones.

Jan Slepian
The Broccoli Tapes

An ache choked him, so that he wanted to put his hand to his throat and tear it out. The beauty of the late March day held only pain to hurt him.

Marjorie Kinnan Rawlings
The Yearling

Over the next several weeks I cried when I came home to silence, when I awoke in the middle of the night to silence, when I got out of bed in the morning to silence. No barking. No skittering toenails on linoleum. No imperious scratching at the door. My warm tears gradually dissolved the spikey chunk of ice lodged high in my belly, until I found at its glacial core the frozen wails, the hidden agony I still felt about the death of my first dog, killed by a truck when I was 11.

I found myself, finally, crying tears that were 40 years old.

Fido would have been 15 had he seen the spring.

I loved him.

Stuart Heller
"Death of a Friend"

I just broke down, and Papa let me cry it all out. I just sobbed and sobbed with my head up toward the sky and my eyes closed, hoping God would hear it.

Robert Newton Peck
A Day No Pigs Would Die

He died that night, and I cried for a week. Papa tried to make me feel better by promising to get me another dog right away, but I wouldn't have it. It made me mad just to think about some other dog's trying to take Bell's place.

Fred Gipson
Old Yeller

I buried Little Ann by the side of Old Dan.

I knew that was where she wanted to be.

I also buried a part of my life along with my dog.

Wilson Rawls
Where the Red Fern Grows

I put Algernon's body into a small metal container and took him home with me.
I wasn't going to let them dump him into the incinerator.
It's foolish and sentimental, but late last night I buried him in the back yard.
I wept as I put a bunch of wild flowers on the grave.

Daniel Keyes
Flowers for Algernon

The waves wash in and over me, but they do not drown me.
Each wave of emotion is, in fact, healing me.

Carol Staudacher
A Time to Grieve

Time cannot steal the treasures you carry in your heart.

What you once enjoyed, you can never lose.

All that you loved becomes a part of you.

Earl A. Grollman
Straight Talk about Death for Teenagers

"What we have to do now is to find a way we can remember her and her beauty. That way we'll have her inside of us. The memories can help us grow. We need that, Aarvy, because you and I are alive. We have to remember that, and not be ashamed."

Donna O'Toole
Aarvy Aardvark Finds Hope

Someday I'll have another dog,
or a kitten or a goldfish,
But whatever it is, I'll tell it
every night: "I'll always love you."

Hans Wilhelm
I'll Always Love You

Name pink panther   **Kennel #** N/A
Age Under 6 Months   **Color** , Black
Breed Domestic Short Hair & Unknown

Pink Panther is a cute cuddly solid black 3 month young kitten looking for her forever home. She is very social and friendly to everyone, cats, kittens and people of all ages. If you are looking for your next best friend, look no more she is it!

Name MT   **Kennel #** N/A
Age Under 6 Months **Color** Black/White
Breed Domestic Medium Hair & Unknown

MT didn't Triumph! is a handsome little 2 month young Tuxedo guy. MT loves to romp and play with other kittens, cats and all people. He does need to be in a home with another kitty or stay at home person as he loves great comfort or companionship - not to mention having someone to play with to that someone you?

Name Montana   **Kennel #** N/A
Age Under 6 Months **Color** Black/White
Breed Domestic Short Hair & Unknown

Montana has a shiny black and white coat with adorable markings. Her mesmerizing eyes will definitely draw you into her spell. She is a friendly kitty who enjoys being petted and will reward all of your attention with lots of rumbling purrs. At 6 months young, Montana is a very playful cat. She loves to chase after the yarn wand or run around with a toy mouse. If you want to bring a little companion into your life she is great with other cats and dogs too.

Name Taz   **Kennel #** N/A
Age Adult **Color** Orange/White
Pattern Tabby
Breed Domestic Short Hair & Unknown

Taz is a 5 year young male. He's a giant teddy bear of a cat (13+ pounds but no fat) and is the sweetest animal I've ever known. He loves attention and will follow you around or just lay with you. And he's equally attentive to other dogs, cats, laying in at the bins. He likes to "talk" right when he wakes up or walks into a room.

Name Alina   **Kennel #** N/A
Age Young Adult **Color** White/Mixed
Breed Domestic Short Hair & Unknown

Hi there – my name is Alina (short hair brown tabby with a white chest, female about 1 1/2 years old. Very sweet natured, I just love being brushed and cuddled. I would love to have a playmate. I am full polite, and it can be another cat, dog, child, they all home an adult. Do I mention I love everyone? Why not come on down and meet me today. I would love to meet you so we can start that forever friendship.

Name Hello Darkness   **Kennel #** N/A
Age Under 6 Months **Color** Black
Breed Domestic Short Hair & Unknown

Hello Darkness is a gorgeous sleek solid black kitten. He is about 5 months young and is a playful young guy who gets distracted at all cats of any type and all people to boot! Hello Darkness will make a wonderful addition to the right family, is that family yours?

Name Sally Jo   **Kennel #** N/A
Age Young Adult **Color** Brown
Pattern Tabby
Breed Domestic Short Hair & Unknown

Hi! My name is Sally Jo, right now I am in foster care. I am the cutest tortoise mix only 4 years young, who is loving and playful with people, cats, and dogs of all shapes and sizes. I have a very calm disposition, and love to eat – shhh... don't tell anyone but if I had cable TV in my room, I'd watch the Food Channel all the time. The other night I heard my foster mom talking on the phone. I can hardly wait to meet and be with my future family.

Name Fisher   **Kennel #** N/A
Age Young Adult **Color** Mixed
Pattern Tortie
Breed Domestic Short Hair & Unknown

Fisher is a 2 year young Tortie Shell who is a total love bug. Fisher came to Cat Connection declawed. She always wants to be on your lap and next to you if you want her. She is also a great lap cat who would be a perfect addition to a household with a few cats, or one could be a well cat, who needs a lot of attention. She is ready to add that special spark in your family – come and meet Fisher.

Name Sun   **Kennel #** N/A
Age Under 6 Months **Color** Brown/Gray
Pattern Tabby
Breed Domestic Short Hair & Unknown

Sun is a 4 month young female gray tabby with beautiful big green eyes. Needs a loving home with lots of huge that she can give in require she is ready to romp and play with everyone-cats, kittens and people of all ages. Are you ready to open your heart to this sweetheart?

Name Phantom   **Kennel #** N/A
Age Under 6 Months **Color** Brown
Pattern Tabby
Breed Domestic Long Hair & Unknown

I am a cute cuddly little 4 month young brown long hair tabby who is looking for a loving home with lots of hugs to give. Playful and energetic, I get along great with other cats, kittens and people of all ages. Do you have a football lying somewhere around your house, I bet I can find it for you? Ready for your best new friend?

Name Apple   **Kennel #** N/A
Age Under 6 Months **Color** Gray
Pattern Solid
Breed Russian Blue & Unknown

Hi I'm Apple! At 4 months of age, I am quite a little mink who loves to play with everyone, cats and people a like. Aren't I cute?! I love people and whenever a human of any age is nearby, I lay by extra onto their lap and put my paws on their shoulders to drink in all the love I can't find a classic little girl looking for my real home. Is it you?

Name green   **Kennel #** N/A
Age Under 6 Months **Color** White
Pattern Spotted
Breed Domestic Short Hair & Unknown

Green is a typical energetic playful 5 month young solid white kitten who needs to go to a home where there are plenty of other toys to entertain her as well as another kitty to play with toys to entertain her. Green is an absolute beauty who home person for company! Green is an absolute beauty who will make a great addition to the right person home.

Being responsible for an animal's life again can be a good experience.
Death should not scare us away from new life.

Wallace Sife
The Loss of a Pet

Another cat? Perhaps. For love there is also a season; its seeds must be resown.
But a family cat is not replaceable like a worn-out coat or a set of tires.
Each new kitten becomes its own cat, and none is repeated.
I am four cats old, measuring out my life in friends that
have succeeded but not replaced one another.

Irving Townsend
Separate Lifetimes

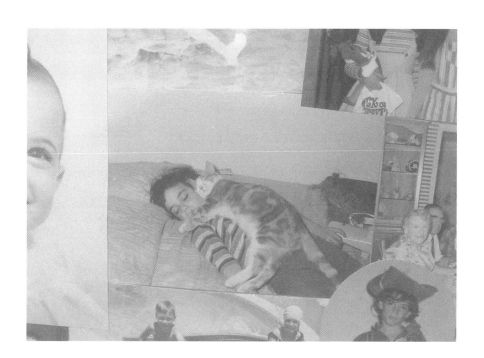

"Men," said Mr. Kyle, "people have been trying to understand dogs ever since the beginning of time. One never knows what they'll do. You can read every day where a dog saved the life of a drowning child, or lay down his life for his master. Some people call this loyalty. I don't. I may be wrong, but I call it love—the deepest kind of love."

Wilson Rawls
Where the Red Fern Grows

"Saying goodbye doesn't mean you have to forget Clarice, Aarvy," Ralphy said gently.

"It means you accept what is. Then you'll be free to remember without it hurting so much. By letting go of Clarice you'll find you have more energy for living. You might even find that saying goodbye helps you love yourself and others more than before. I think Clarice would like that, Aarvy."

Donna O'Toole
Aarvy Aardvark Finds Hope

"It just seems so wrong to love and be happy after someone you loved so much dies," she said softly, the tears welling up again. She turned away, facing the wall so Devin wouldn't see her cry.

"Why does it seem so wrong? Consider this: do we really honor someone's memory–even a horse's memory–by being miserable for the rest of our lives? Aren't there better ways to honor someone you loved?"

Karle Dickerson
The Forgotten Filly

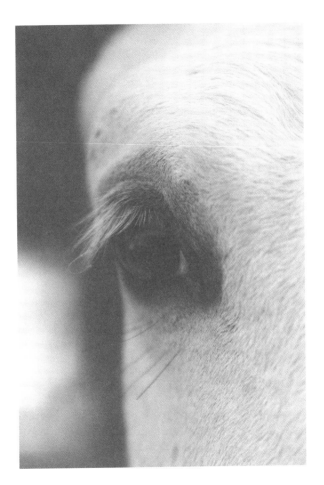

Wilbur never forgot Charlotte.
Although he loved her children and grandchildren dearly,
none of the new spiders ever quite took her place in his heart.
She was in a class by herself. It is not often that someone comes along
who is a true friend and a good writer. Charlotte was both.

E.B. White
Charlotte's Web

I will not equate the length of my grieving period with the degree of my love. One has nothing to do with the other. I will cry until I no longer need to cry, will grieve until I no longer need to grieve. And through it all, my love will continue unchanged and undiminished.

Carol Staudacher
A Time to Grieve

I do believe that we and our animals will meet again.
If we do not, and where we go is supposed to be heaven,
it will not be heaven to me and it will not be where I wish to go.

Cleveland Amory
The Best Cat Ever

Cooper's tremendous love and energy and unchained freedom had captured life itself. Now, as the last shovelful covered him forever, I knew I would always carry a big piece of Cooper Half Malamute with me until I too was covered by the earth.

Peter Jenkins
A Walk Across America

"Every animal you met there is in a story.
The stories are all written now;
they had their beginnings, their middles,
and their ends, but now they are complete.
That's where their lives are–in those stories.
But those stories can happen again and those
animals can have their lives over again every
time a human sits down to read."

Dennis Hamley
Hare's Choice

One last word of farewell, Dear Master and Mistress. Whenever you visit my grave,
say to yourselves with regret but also with happiness in your hearts
at the remembrance of my long happy life with you:
"Here lies one who loved us and whom we loved."
No matter how deep my sleep I shall hear you,
and not all the power of death can keep
my spirit from wagging a grateful tail.

Eugene O'Neill
The Last Will and Testament of an Extremely Distinguished Dog

Resolution is the knitting up of open wounds, but there will always be a secret scar. It is the taking of a brave step forward, putting things into new harmony. This is finally the time for letting go. That means allowing the focus of emotion and attention to be shifted, permitting us to continue with our own life's growth. This is when our pain changes from an immobilizing force to one of precious remembrance, hope and self-regeneration.

Our life goes on, but we never let go of the love that still is so cherished. It becomes a fundamental passion within us, never to be lost.

Wallace Sife
The Loss of a Pet

We who choose to surround ourselves with lives even more temporary
than our own live within a fragile circle, easily and often breached.
Unable to accept its awful gaps, we still would live no other way.
We cherish memory as the only certain immortality,
never fully understanding the necessary plan.

Irving Townsend
Separate Lifetimes

Living beyond the deaths of my animal companions,

I learned that time softens the hurt and sweetens the memories.

And as my animal companions have returned to live again in my dreams

and in my heart, I am reminded over and over that love doesn't know death.

Susan Chernak McElroy
Animals as Teachers & Healers

Where he is really buried, and where he is, and where he will always be, is in my heart.

Cleveland Amory
The Best Cat Ever

The Fur Person closed his eyes and sang his song and it went like this:

Thank you, thank you,
You and no other
Dear gentle voice,
Dear human mother,
For your delicate air,
For your *savoir-faire*
For your kind soft touch
Thank you very much.

May Sarton
The Fur Person

September/October, 1991, p. 15. Reprinted with permission of *NEXUS Magazine*. *A Day No Pigs Would Die* by Robert Newton Peck. Copyright © 1972 by Robert Newton Peck. Reprinted by permission of Random House Children's Books, a division of Random House, Inc. *Flowers for Algernon* by Daniel Keyes. Copyright © 1959, 1966 by Daniel Keyes. Published by Harcourt, Inc. *Straight Talk about Death for Teenagers: How to Cope with Losing Someone You Love* by Earl A. Grollman. Copyright © 1993 by Earl A. Grollman. Published by Beacon Press. *A Time to Grieve: Meditations for Healing After the Death of a Loved One* by Carol Staudacher. Copyright © 1994 by Carol Staudacher. Reprinted by permission of HarperCollins Publishers. *Aarvy Aardvark Finds Hope* by Donna O'Toole. Text and art copyright © 1988 by Donna O'Toole. Published by Compassion Press and available in book and video at Compassion Books, Inc., 7036 State Highway 80 South, Burnsville, NC 28714 or from their website at www.compassionbooks.com. *I'll Always Love You* by Hans Wilhelm. Copyright © 1985 by Hans Wilhelm, Inc. Reprinted by permission of Random House Children's Books, a division of Random House, Inc. *Separate Lifetimes* by Irving Townsend. Reprinted with permission from the publisher Flying Dog Press, P.O. Box 105, St. Johnsville, NY 13452, (800) 7-FLY-DOG, www.flyingdogpress.com. *The Forgotten Filly* by Karle Dickerson. Copyright © 1993 by Daniel Weiss Associates, Inc. and Karle Dickerson. HarperCollins Publishers. *Charlotte's Web* by E.B. White. Copyright 1952 by E.B. White. Text copyright renewed 1980 by E.B. White. Used by permission of HarperCollins Publishers. *A Walk Across America* by Peter Jenkins. Copyright © 1979 by Peter Jenkins. Reprinted by permission of HarperCollins Publishers, William Morrow. *The Last Will and Testament of an Extremely Distinguished Dog* by Eugene O'Neill. Henry Holt and Company, LLC.

Our deepest thanks to those who allowed us to photograph them and/or their pets: Juan and Kim Balbuena; the Dreyer family; Melissa Farnsworth; Lexi Kotler; Ann Milligan Lees; Amir Mathis; Carol McKee Rosinski; and Zak Shaffer. Our additional gratitude to the following persons who contributed their support and their family photos: Emiliano Almeida; Germán Krebs; Aaron, Marissa and Liana Lahann; and Ann Milligan Lees.

About the Author
Laynee Gilbert, M.A., is a counselor and writer. Other books to her credit include *Pass It On: Ultimate Reflections on Life and Death*; *I Remember You: A Grief Journal*; and *The Complete Dream Journal.* To learn more about the author and her books, go to www.loapublications.com.

About the Photographer
Marcie Gilbert is a photographer, teacher, and the author of the children's picture book, *Zee... Adventure One: Borrowing China.* Other credits include *Pass It On: Ultimate Reflections on Life and Death*. Visit her websites at www.marciegilbert.com and www.librujas.com.

About the Designer
Patricia Krebs is a visual artist, musician, and the illustrator of the children's picture book, *Zee... Adventure One: Borrowing China.* Other credits include *Pass It On: Ultimate Reflections on Life and Death.* See her works at www.patriciakrebs.com.ar and www.librujas.com.